yo!

ANCIENT ASTRONAUTS

ANCIENT ASTRONAUTS

by Ian Thorne

Illustrations by
Barbara Howell Furan

Library of Congress Catalog Card Number: 78-7973

International Standard Book Numbers:
    0-913940-86-0 Library Bound
    0-89686-007-8 Paperback

Edited by - Dr. Howard Schroeder
            Prof. in Reading and Language Arts
            Dept. of Elementary Education
            Mankato State University

Layout and Design - Barb Furan

Astronaut Jack R. Lousma, Skylab 3 pilot.

Library of Congress
Cataloging in Publication Data

Thorne, Ian.
  Ancient Astronauts.

  (Search for the Unknown)
  SUMMARY: Discusses Swiss writer Erich von Daniken's theories concerning extraterrestrial influences on the development of ancient civilizations.
  1. Civilization, Ancient--Extraterrestrial influences-- Juvenile literature. (1. Civilization, Ancient--Extrater- restrial influences) I. Furan, Barbara Howell. II. Title.
  CB156.T48   001.9'42   78-7973
  ISBN 0-913940-86-0

ANCIENT
ASTRONAUTS

EARTH MYSTERIES

We are people of the Space Age.

Astronauts have gone to the Moon, and have taken pictures of Earth from outer space. We can see that it is really a small planet — one of many millions in the vast universe.

But, the earth is ours, we want to know more about it, and about the human race living upon it. People ask questions, such as:

Where did the human race come from?

Were human beings born on Earth — or did they come here from another planet?

Are we the only thinking people in the universe, or are there many intelligent races?

Did visitors from space come to earth in the distant past? Is it possible we are visited by people from other worlds today?

If people from other worlds visited Earth, did they leave a trace of their coming?

If people from other worlds visited Earth, did they have contact with ancient humans?

The planet Earth, seen from space, looks very small. Scientists tell us Earth is about 5 billion years old. Some believe "modern" man has only lived on the planet for half a million years. Written history goes back only a few thousand years.

Finding an answer to these questions is not easy.

We cannot look for too many answers in history books. Written history goes back only about 4,500 years, and many ancient people did not have a writing system.

If we want to find out about ancient people, we must study the things they left behind — things such as bones, pottery, art works, buildings, etc. As we study these things, we find many mysteries.

The science that studies cultures without a written history is called archaeology. These archaeologists are uncovering a village that dates back to the times of Joseph (1700 B.C.) in Bethel, Jordan.

The statues of Easter Island in the South Pacific are up to 40 feet tall. Some of them weigh 70 tons. Ever since the island was discovered in 1722, scientists have argued about who made the statues — and how.

Travel around the world, and you will see some mysteries of the past. You'll see things made by ancient people, and you will wonder how they made them. How did people without modern tools make things like the —

pyramids of Egypt?
huge statues of Easter Island?
abandoned cities of Mexico?
giant pictures on the desert of Peru?

The pyramids at Giza have mystified tourists for thousands of years. They were built between 2500 and 2600 B. C.

Some day you may take a trip to Egypt. Outside the big city of Cairo, Egypt is one of the best-known of the ancient mysteries. There we find the three great pyramids of Giza.

The largest is the Great Pyramid of King Khufu. It towers 450 feet high and its square base covers 13 acres. It is huge — a mountain made of blocks of stone. More than two million blocks, each weighing about two-and-a-half tons, were used to make the Great Pyramid.

There is something very mysterious about the Great Pyramid. It seems to frighten some people. The Great Pyramid was ancient when Christ was born. People of Julius Caesar's time called it one of the Seven Wonders of the World.

Could mere men have built such a thing? Primitive men, with simple tools? Modern engineers with the best machinery would hardly be able to build such a pyramid today.

The pyramids are just one of the ancient mysteries. There are many others as well. For years, scientists have tried to explain them, but have not always agreed on their explanations. Some of the "answers" to ancient mysteries have later been proved to be wrong.

This has made some people doubt that we know the truth about mankind's past. One of these doubters is a Swiss writer named Erich von Däniken. He became world-famous when he said "gods from outer space," ancient astronauts, visited Earth long ago. Von Däniken said the pyramids, the Easter Island statues, and other mystery objects appeared to be traces of these visitors.

Erich von Däniken (right) was born in Switzerland in 1935. Before writing his famous book, he was the manager of a hotel. He had no scientific training.

Erich von Däniken began to write a book about ancient visitors from outer space. He borrowed some of his ideas from other writers, and studied books on archaeology, the science that studies man's past. He also studied books on modern space science.

Von Däniken finished his first book in 1966. It was a time when UFOs (Unidentified Flying Objects) were being reported in many parts of the world. People seemed to be seeing flying saucers everywhere.

At that time American and Soviet space craft were making trips into outer space. The whole world was interested in space travel. For that reason von Däniken's book about ancient astronauts did not seem unbelievable.

In the United States the book was called **Chariots of the Gods.** It became a best-seller.

In 1965, Gemini IV astronaut James McDivitt saw a strange cylinder with an "antenna" while he was traveling in space. This UFO has never been satisfactorily explained.

SPACE GODS

Just about the time von Däniken's book came out, a movie appeared. It, too, had a theme of ancient astronauts visiting Earth.

The movie was **2001: A Space Odyssey.** It became one of the most popular movies of all time. In it, man-apes found a strange, black thing. It had been sent to Earth by powerful beings from another world.

The man-apes in the movie were supposed to be our ancestors. They were puzzled by the black thing. Their minds worked slowly. But then one man-ape touched the thing. ZAP! The ape instantly became smarter!

The black thing was a kind of teaching-machine. Through it, the man-ape learned to use a tool. He picked up a bone and used it to kill with.

The movie seemed to be telling us that ancient man-apes needed help from outer space in order to begin thinking like true human beings.

Von Däniken's **Chariots of the Gods** said just about the same thing. The book spoke of god-legends. Many groups of people have old stories of gods who came from the sky in fiery chariots. To von Däniken, these "chariots" were really space craft, and the "gods," themselves, were really ancient astronauts.

*Man-apes in **2001: A Space Odyssey** were mere animals until the black "teaching-machine" slab gave them human intelligence.*

American astronauts on the Moon did not report any signs of life.

Von Däniken wrote other books using the same ideas. In 1973, a TV special based on **Chariots of the Gods** was shown. It was called, "In Search of Ancient Astronauts." Millions of people in the United States, Canada, and elsewhere saw it. They found von Däniken's ideas to be interesting so they bought his books and read more about them.

Meanwhile, real astronauts walked on the moon, and UFOs kept appearing in the skies. People in all walks of life claimed to have seen them — policemen, homemakers, airline pilots, students, even a governor.

By the 1970's, nearly half the people in the United States thought UFOs were real, and that they came from outer space. So Erich von Däniken's ideas did not seem silly at all.

If UFOs could visit Earth in the 1970's, why couldn't they have come long ago?

Von Däniken gathered all kinds of "proof" that ancient astronauts had come to Earth. He showed the picture seen below. It is a carving from the lid of a tomb in Palenque, Mexico. The tomb was built by the ancient Maya people in the year 683 A.D.

Von Däniken stated, "any child can see the man in the picture is sitting inside a rocket. He is lying back as modern astronauts do. He is working with the 'controls' of a space ship. At the bottom are 'flames' from the rocket's exhaust."

Mayan ruins at Uxmal, in Mexico's Yucatan Peninsula, are only one part of the wide-flung "empire" of this ancient civilization. The Mayas were powerful from about A.D. 350 until about 1450. When Spanish explorers came to America, the Maya civilization had declined.

Von Däniken seems to believe the Mayas were primitive jungle people until they were visited by space travelers. The beings from space are supposed to have taught the Mayas many kinds of wonderful things and, as a result, they became a great nation.

The Mayas built grand cities and temples in the forests of Mexico, Guatemala, and Honduras. They had a calendar, symbols for writing, and could do complex mathematics. They also studied the movements of the stars and planets, and worshipped a god, Kukulkan, the plumed serpent, who was believed to have come from the stars.

Erich von Däniken said that he found traces of ancient astronauts in many parts of the world. This drawing, from a rock wall at Tassili in the Sahara Desert of Africa, shows a figure 18 feet tall. It was made by very early artists.

Von Däniken believed that the figure looked like a helmeted spaceman.

Von Däniken looked at drawings made by the primitive people of Australia. Wodjina, a goddess without a mouth, seemed to him to be a space visitor. An Indian rock painting from California also looked like a spaceman to him.

Many primitive artists have shown people wearing horned headgear. To von Däniken, the horns were radio antennae. Other ancient artwork shows masked figures, which von Däniken interpreted as beings from other worlds, using breathing equipment.

Many Indian drawings resemble this one, from China Lake, California, which some people think represents an ancient spaceman.

Right: a modern astronaut in his spacesuit looks a little like the ancient cavedrawing.

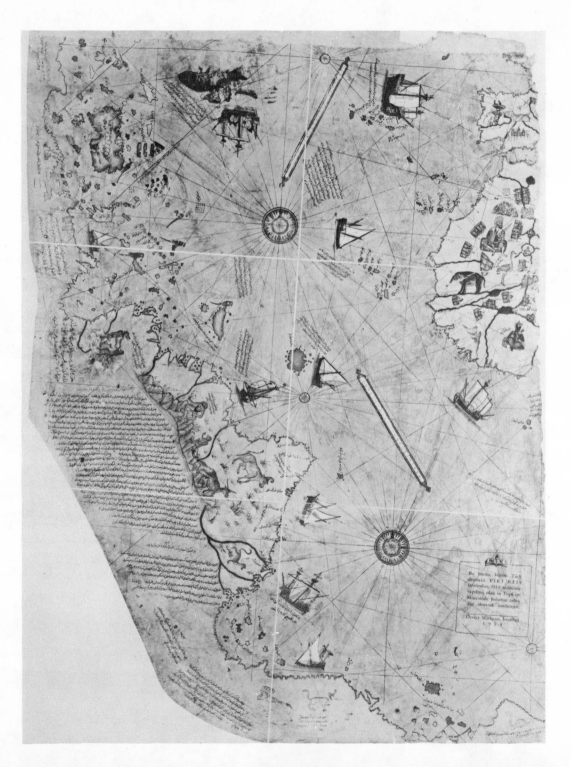

Von Däniken argued that the ancient Egyptians could not have built the pyramids without help from ancient astronauts. He said the Egyptians could not have cut the huge stone blocks and moved them by themselves.

He also claimed the ancient people of Easter Island could not have made the giant statues without astronaut aid. How could the people have cut the rock? How could they have set up statues weighing many tons? These questions remain unanswered.

It seemed that everywhere he looked, von Däniken found traces of ancient astronauts. He studied an old map made by the Turkish admiral, Piri Reis, in 1513.

Von Däniken said: "Antarctica, mapped at the bottom, conforms very closely to the land mass under the ice, as revealed by echo-sounding gear."

The old Turks certainly did not have such gear, therefore, "the map must have been made with the most modern technical aid from the air." Von Däniken decided that the Piri Reis map must have been made by spacemen orbiting the world long ago!

One of von Däniken's most famous "ancient mysteries" lies in the South American country of Peru.

The Piri Reis map, according to von Däniken, is "too accurate" to have been made by 16th century Earth people. Could the Turkish admiral have based his map on a chart taken from ancient astronauts?

There on a desert plain near Nazca are giant patterns, traced in the soil and rock. A person standing on the ground can hardly tell the patterns are there.

However, if you fly above the desert in an airplane, you see that the plain is criss-crossed by many straight lines. They look like outlines of airport runways. The Nazca plain also has outlines of huge birds, fish, a lizard, a monkey with a coiled tail, a spider, and other creatures.

Seen from the ground, the Nazca patterns are barely visible.

Seen from the air, the Nazca patterns look like they were carefully drawn by a giant artist. The lines are perfectly straight, and it is difficult to believe that most primitive people would be able to draw straight lines with the few instruments which were available to them.

The Nazca patterns may be as much as 2,400 years old. Why were they made? Who made them? Archaeologists have asked these questions ever since the patterns were discovered.

Erich von Däniken said the Nazca lines were a signal to ancient astronauts and meant, "Land here!" He suggested that some of the lines appeared to be landing strips for space craft.

In his many books, von Däniken cited "evidence" of ancient astronauts all over the world.

The ancient Egyptian sun god, Ra, has a winged disk as his symbol. The ancient Sumerians, Assyrians and Mayas also use winged figures of gods. The Bible makes reference to angels which are often pictured as winged beings.

To von Däniken, all of these refer to ancient astronauts. Every legend of sky gods is, to him, a "memory" of people from outer space who once visited Earth, did good or evil things, then went back to their homes on distant planets. In his mind the human race owes its progress to the help given long ago by visitors from outer space.

Ashur, war god of the Assyrians, is shown riding in a winged disk. This carving was made about 800 B. C.

CHARIOTS UNDER FIRE

More books about ancient astronauts were written. TV programs and movies about the subject were made. Some people became confused. Were there really such things as ancient astronauts? Was Erich von Däniken right when he said ancient human beings could not have made mysterious things like the pyramids?

Almost every scientist said von Däniken's ideas were nonsense. But that wasn't good enough. Scientists had been saying for years that flying saucers and other UFOs were nonsense, too. Yet, people kept on seeing them!

It was not enough to say that von Däniken's ideas were untrue. Scientists were asked to prove them. The evidence would have to come not only from space scientists, but from archaeologists, too.

For example, how can the huge Easter Island statues be explained? If they are not images of space-people, cut from the rock with laser tools and set up with the help of ancient astronauts, then what are they?

The question was studied in 1955 by Thor Heyerdahl and others. An account of their scientific expedition to Easter Island is told in the book, **Aku-Aku.**

Thor Heyerdahl made friends with the people living on Easter Island. They told him, and showed him, how the huge statues were made.

There are still stone quarries on Easter Island. They contain half-finished statues. And they have hundreds of teardrop-shaped hand-picks made of harder stone.

In **Chariots of the Gods** von Däniken calls the rock the statues are carved from "steel-hard." But it is not really very hard at all, and if you put water on it, it becomes rather soft.

The Easter Island people of 1955 showed Heyerdahl how a statue could be carved. At the rate they worked, it would take about a year for two teams of six men to finish a medium-sized statue.

Von Däniken said no large trees ever grew on Easter Island which means people could not have used log rollers to move the statues.

Is it true large trees never grew on the island? If it were true, then islanders used a different way to move the statues. They put the statues on wooden sleds, made from smaller logs. Then they pulled the sleds with ropes. Modern Easter Island people pulled a 12-ton statue along in this manner for Thor Heyerdahl.

And how were the statues set up? The islanders showed Heyerdahl how to do that, too.

As the statue is levered higher and higher, more stones are shoved under it, making a ramp-like pile. After a time, the statue settles upright and the stone pile can be taken away. Archaeologists agree that this could be the way the ancient Easter Island people erected the statues. The last of the old statues was carved about 1680. They were monuments for dead chiefs.

This scale model from the Boston Museum of Science shows ancient Egyptians building the pyramid of King Menkaure. At the bottom, men are hauling a stone block on a wooden sled. Log rollers beneath help move the stone easily.

The pyramids of ancient Egypt are amazing. But they are not so amazing that space visitors are needed to explain them.

Von Däniken could not believe the Egyptians did the work themselves. He could not understand how the ancient people could level the ground under the pyramid. He did not believe the Egyptians could cut the stone blocks, or bring them from the quarry to the pyramid site. Archaeologists say the stone blocks were probably carried on log rollers. But von Däniken believes the Egyptians had no large logs.

Archaeologists say it is simply not true that we lack the understanding of how the pyramids were built. Von Däniken's wonder over the greatness of the pyramids has caused him to ignore ideas suggested by archaeologists.

The stone blocks were cut with tools of hard stone. The Egyptians also used fire and water to aid in cracking rock. Like the people of Easter Island, they used long poles as levers. These helped place the stones on wooden sleds.

The pyramid was built slowly. All men in the kingdom had to work on the project for several months each year. A wide ramp wound around the pyramid as it grew taller. It formed a roadway for workmen. King Menkaure's pyramid was built about 2525 B. C.

33

Von Däniken may also be wrong about the Egyptians not having logs for rollers. It is true that large trees did not grow in Egypt, but they did grow in Lebanon. Cedar logs from Lebanon could have been transported to Egypt by ship. Egyptian writings tell us about this trade.

The Egyptians could have leveled the site for the pyramids with water! The surface of water is always perfectly flat. Archaeologists say that Egyptian engineers might have built a low dike in the square where the pyramid was to be. They could flood this with shallow water. Then they could dig away the ground below, until the water was the same depth all over. When the water was drained off, the level pyramid site would be ready.

Another of von Däniken's "proofs" of ancient astronauts is the Piri Reis map.

In **Chariots of the Gods** he stated that the map is "absolutely accurate." He says the map shows the South American coast in a "precise" way.

Look again at the Piri Reis map, on page 22 of this book. In his book, **In Search of Ancient Astronauts,** von Däniken says there are minimal errors in the map, which means he believes there are hardly any errors at all.

But compare the Piri Reis map with a modern map of the Caribbean Sea. Do the two maps look alike? Of course, they don't. Piri has made several errors in drawing the islands in the Caribbean.

MODERN MAP OF THE CARIBBEAN AREA

Next look at Piri's coast of South America. (See map on page 22). Like many old map-makers, Piri has left out parts. In other cases, he has put in parts that don't exist.

Erich von Däniken says the lower part of the map plainly shows Antarctica "without the ice." But if you peel off the Ronne Shelf Ice just below South America, you would have a vast bay just east of the Antarctic Peninsula. It would not look like the Piri Reis map at all.

If ancient astronauts made Piri's map, as von Däniken says, then they apparently made several mistakes.

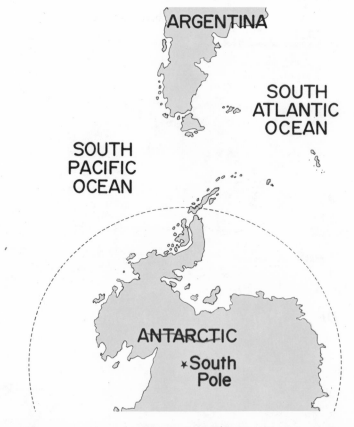

MODERN MAP OF SOUTHERN SOUTH AMERICA AND THE COAST OF ANTARCTICA

Von Däniken likes to use Latin American archaeology to "prove" his theories. The "Mayan astronaut" of Palenque impresses many people. Look at his picture again. It is on page 18.

Von Däniken believes "any child" can see that the man is sitting inside a rocket. Is this really true? If it is, then why is the man's head poking outside his "space ship?"

If you look carefully at the nose of the Mayan "rocket," you will see a bird sitting on it. It is a Quetzal, a bird sacred to the Mayas.

Did Mayan rockets have hood ornaments?

Von Däniken thinks the man's clothes are "appropriate" for an astronaut. Yet anyone can see the man is wearing anklets, bracelets, and beads around his neck. He is naked except for the kilt that wealthy Mayans wore. His feet are bare.

Most people would say this man was dressed for life in a hot jungle, not for space travel.

Archaeologists think this tomb-lid carving showed a Mayan ruler just after death. He is rising toward the Mayan heaven, where the holy bird awaits. The lower part of the carving represents the earth. The upper part is the spirit world.

Do you think this explanation is better than von Däniken's?

An Apollo lunar lander has no wheels or wings. It rests on legs, which can be pulled back into the ship when it travels through space.

And then there are the ancient astronaut "landing fields" in Peru.

What are the lines on the Nazca Plain? Does it seem reasonable to say they outline runways for space craft?

First of all, a space craft need not be an airplane. Most have no wings or wheels for landing. Many rocket-powered space ships hover above the ground and slowly sink straight down to land. They rest on legs, and most often land in a level place.

The Nazca lines are drawn in soft sand and gravel. Even if the ancient astronauts had "airplane-space-ships," they may have experienced difficulty landing on the Nazca Plain. The lines cross dry creek beds. The landers could have tumbled into them.

There is little doubt the ancient Nazca people worshipped sky gods. Archaeologists believe the lines and the giant pictures are objects of worship. They were intended to be seen by the gods who would be impressed by the work the Nazca people had done. No doubt the Nazca people wanted to please their gods by doing great things. Many believe Christian people of the Middle Ages built beautiful churches for the same reason.

Toltec people of Mexico carved these statues about 900 A.D. Von Däniken thinks that they represent astronauts. He points to the "boxes" on their chests, which he says are like the apparatus of lunar astronauts. Archaeologists say these are statues of warriors. They wear breast-plates in the shape of the Toltec fire-butterfly. Which explanation makes more sense to you?

Gigantic heads such as this one were made by Mexico's Olmec people between 900 and 500 B.C. Von Däniken thinks they show "robots." Archaeologists think an even more interesting mystery lies behind them. The heads have negroid features. And yet there were no black people in Mexico until the 1500's. Or . . . did black explorers from Africa sail to Southern Mexico more than 2000 years ago?

In another "proof" of ancient astronauts, von Däniken speaks of this rustproof iron pillar near Delhi, India. Did scientists from outer space make this pillar? Archaeologists say it was made by clever Indian ironsmiths about 1500 years ago as a memorial to a king. The iron does not rust because it is very pure. Ordinary iron things which rust contain other elements as impurities.

It is logical to think of the Nazca lines as religious artwork. Some archaeologists think they may point to certain stars. The animal pictures may also represent constellations.

The straightness of the lines may be easy to explain. For example, the Nazca people could have stretched long strings across the plains, which would have helped them draw straight lines on the soil.

It appears ancient people were more intelligent than Erich von Däniken believed.

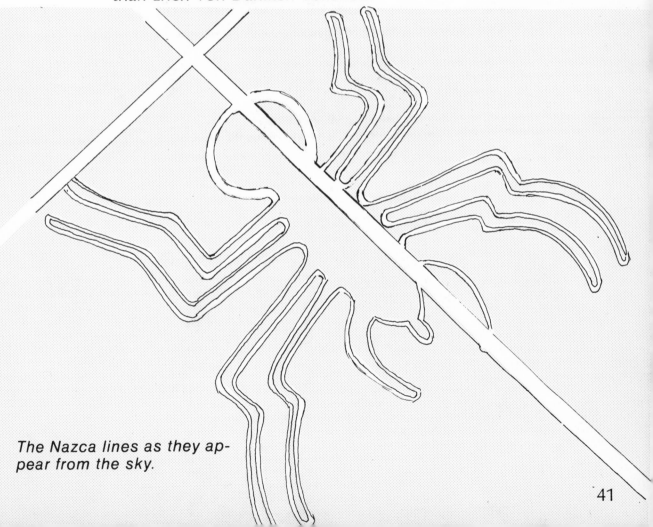

The Nazca lines as they appear from the sky.

ANCIENT ASTRONAUTS

The people who lived thousands of years ago had brains just like ours. They were clever. They could think through problems and find answers to them. They studied the movements of the stars, sun, and moon. Some nations even developed calendars.

Thousands of years ago, ancient engineers built canals to irrigate farms. They built great palaces and temples to their gods. The artists of long ago made statues, jewelry, and other things we admire today.

We do not understand exactly how ancient people accomplished some of the things they did. Slowly the mysteries are being unraveled. Sometimes it takes a person like Thor Heyerdahl to discover a forgotten piece of science. Many scientists, working in different parts of the world, help put the pieces of the puzzle together.

Little by little, our knowledge of the past and its people grows. We are impressed by the things ancient people did and find they were not necessarily ignorant savages.

Ancient people were, at times, very clever and practical. So far, none of the things archaeologists have found appear to be beyond the powers of ancient people. Ancient people may not have needed the help of astronauts to make the pyramids, the Easter Island statues, the rustproof iron pillar of India or any of the other marvelous things that impressed Erich von Däniken.

What about the artwork which is supposed to show ancient astronauts?

Von Däniken's books are full of ancient drawings made by primitive people. Some of them are very crude. They show stick figures with rayed halos about the head. To von Däniken, these are astronauts in space suits and helmets.

But are they? A person with a vivid imagination might find a "spaceman" in this piece of primitive artwork. An archaeologist may say the picture shows the sun god of a tribe in Colombia, South America.

It is not always easy to understand the pictures of ancient people.

This fabric, made about 1400 B.C., forms the figure of the sun god in an abstract way. The god is shown as a symbol, not as a "photographic" image. Many primitive people use symbols in their art. This can confuse people who do not understand the symbols.

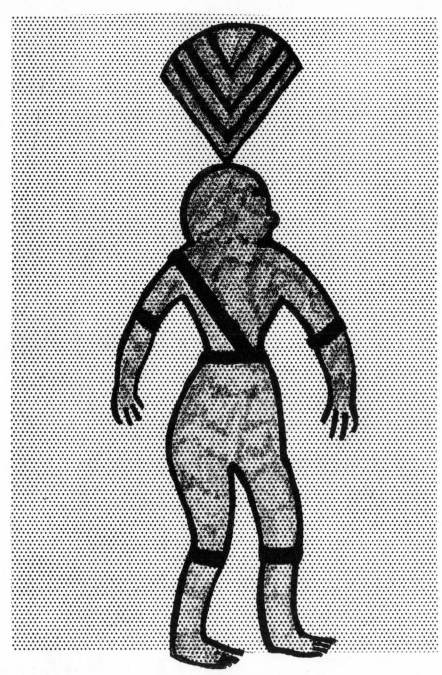

Von Däniken thinks this primitive African rock painting shows an astronaut.

44

So far, there is no definite proof that Earth was visited by ancient astronauts. Erich von Däniken has tried to supply such proof. He is very eager to find ancient astronauts, so appears to find them everywhere.

Again and again, von Däniken implies that primitive people were ignorant. Scientists and historians tell us this is not true. The human race has progressed slowly over a period of many years. The record can be traced. Brains of fossil men became larger and larger. The things they created appear to be proof of this. Human progress may not have required help from outer space.

These models of fossil skulls show how man's brain has grown larger over a period of many years.

APE   **FOSSIL MAN**   **MAN**

Erich von Däniken and the other ancient-astronaut writers have failed to prove their point. However, this does not mean there were no ancient astronauts.

It is quite possible that there are other intelligent beings in the universe. Outer space is a vast place with millions of suns and planets. Some of them may have intelligent life. Space visitors may have been keeping an eye on Earth for a long time.

Would intelligent people from other worlds meddle with human life? That is the question.

Earth people have gone from early stages of development to now exploring space. Tomorrow may hold the answers!

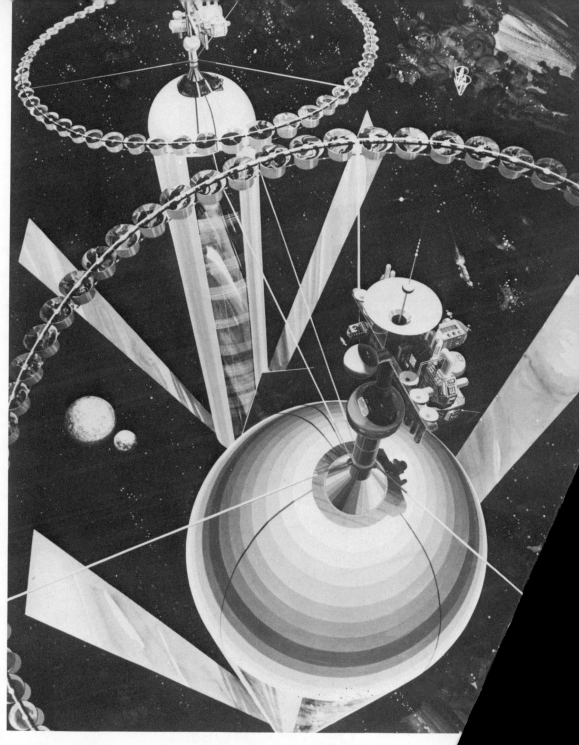

Someday, we will explore the stars in huge space craf[t].
Then we will find out whether or not we are alone in t[he]
universe.

INVESTIGATE THE OTHER FINE BOOKS IN THIS SERIES

CRESTWOOD HOUSE INC.
BOX 3427 MANKATO, MN 56001

47